Piano • Vocal

BROADWAY MUSICALS
Show by Show
1891-1916

D0523135

CONTENTS

Hal Leonard Publishing Corporation

7777 West Bluemound Road P.O. Box 13819 Milwaukee, WI 53213

ISBN 0-7935-0777

Foreword

The Broadway musical, with its combination of music, dancing and visual delights, is truly one of America's great cultural treasures. From the hundreds of productions which have been mounted since 1891, we've selected the best music, and combined it with interesting facts and photographs to create a one-of-a-kind seven-volume songbook series: Broadway Musicals - Show By Show.

About The Author Of The Text

The comments about each show in this collection are excerpted from the book *Broadway Musicals Show by Show* by author Stanley Green. Mr. Green (1923-1990) was highly regarded as one of the leading scholars in the field of musical theatre. His eleven books are among the most widely read on the subject, including *The World of Musical Comedy, The Rodgers and Hammerstein Story, Broadway Musicals of the 30s, Starring Fred Astaire, Encyclopaedia of the Musical Theatre, Encyclopaedia of the Musical Film, The Great Clowns of Broadway, Broadway Musicals Show by Show,* and *Hollywood Musicals Year by Year.* He also compiled and edited *The Rodgers and Hammerstein Fact Book,* the definitive reference on that phenomenally successful collaboration.

Mr. Green was born in New York and lived there throughout his life. He began his writing career as a record reviewer for *Saturday Review,* and later was a contributing editor for *HiFi/Stereo Review.* His articles appeared regularly in such publications as *The New York Times, Musical America, Variety,* and *The Atlantic Monthly.* He worked as a film publicist in New York and London, and was public relations advisor to ASCAP for the years 1961-1965. In 1967 he wrote the script for the revue *Salute to the American Musical Theatre,* first performed at the Waldorf-Astoria, and subsequently presented at the White House on three consecutive evenings. He also wrote the script for "The Music of Kurt Weill" and was music advisor for "Review of Reviews," two programs presented at Lincoln Center in New York.

In 1974, at the request of Richard Rodgers, Mr. Green appeared with the composer on the first videotaped program for the Theatre Collection of the New York Public Library at Lincoln Center. He has been involved with many recording projects, including a 100-record series on Broadway musicals for the Franklin Mint, and the album *Starring Fred Astaire,* which he co-produced for Columbia. In 1987 he moderated a series of seminars marking the 100th birthday of George Abbott. Mr. Green presented many lectures on musical theatre and film at Union College, University of Hartford, New York University, C. W. Post College, Lincoln Center Library, Goodspeed Opera, and Marymount College. He continued to be active as a writer and researcher until the time of his death in December of 1990.

ROBIN HOOD

Music:
Reginald KeKoven

Lyrics & book:
Harry B. Smith

Producer:
The Bostonians

Director:
Harry Dixon

Cast:
Tom Karl, Eugene Cowles, Caroline Hamilton, Jessie Bartlett Davis, W.H. MacDonald, Henry Clay Barnabee, George Frothingham

Songs:
**"Song of Brown October Ale";
"Oh, Promise Me!" (lyric: Clement Scott);
"Tinkers' Chorus";
"Ah, I Do Love Thee"**

New York run:
Standard Theatre, September 28, 1891; 40 p.

*T*he most celebrated American operetta of the 19th century, *Robin Hood* was produced by a touring company that first presented it in Chicago in June 1890. Though hastily put together at a total cost of $109.50, the musical caught on and was remounted in a more stylish production. It made an auspicious New York bow at the Standard Theatre (then on Broadway at 32nd Street), but its run was cut short because of a prior booking. Eight revivals were shown in the city, the last in 1944.

The story remains faithful to the familiar legend about Robin and his merry band of altruistic outlaws who dwell in Sherwood Forest and take from the have-lots and give to the have-nots. In addition to Robin's beloved Maid Marian, the well-known characters include Little John, Friar Tuck, Will Scarlet, and Alan-a-Dale (a traditionally female part originated by Jessie Bartlett Davis, who scored a hit singing the interpolated "Oh, Promise Me!"). This was the third musical created by the team of Reginald DeKoven and Harry B. Smith, who collaborated on a total of 17, including the unsuccessful sequel, *Maid Marian*.

A TRIP TO CHINATOWN

Music:
Percy Gaunt

Lyrics:
Percy Gaunt & Charles H. Hoyt

Book:
Charles H. Hoyt

Producer:
Charles H. Hoyt

Directors:
Charles H. Hoyt & Julian Mitchell

Cast:
Anna Boyd, Lloyd Wilson, George Beane Jr., Lillian Barr, Harry Conor

Songs:
**"Reuben and Cynthia"; "The Bowery"; "Push Dem Clouds Away"; "After the Ball"
(Charles K. Harris)**

New York run:
**Madison Square Theatre,
November 9, 1891; 657 p.**

*I*n a large American city at the turn of the century, two young couples are encouraged by a coquettish widow to defy a rich merchant by having a merry night on the town at a fashionable restaurant. Complications arise when the merchant also shows up at the restaurant and is stuck with their bill — which he cannot pay because he doesn't have his wallet. If this outline reads like the plot of *Hello, Dolly!,* well it is. It is also the plot of *A Trip to Chinatown,* which came along 73 years earlier and which also set a long-running record for continuous performances. In fact, its tenure at the Madison Square Theatre (formerly the Fifth Avenue) was so extraordinary for its time that the show held the durability record for 28 years.

A Trip to Chinatown (though set in San Francisco, no one takes a trip anywhere near Chinatown) was the creation of Charles H. Hoyt, a prolific writer of American farces. It was also the first musical to boast no less than three song hits: "Reuben and Cynthia," "The Bowery," and the interpolated "After the Ball."

THE FORTUNE TELLER

Music:
Victor Herbert

Lyrics & book:
Harry B. Smith

Producer:
Frank L. Perley

Director:
Julian Mitchell

Cast:
**Alice Nielsen, Eugene Cowles,
Frank Rushworth, Marguerite Silva, Joseph
Herbert, Joseph Cawthorn, May Boley**

Songs:
**"Always Do as People Say You Should";
"Romany Life";
"Gypsy Love Song";
"Czardas";
"Only in the Play"**

New York run:
Wallack's Theatre, September 26, 1898; 40 p.

*L*ike *Robin Hood, The Fortune Teller* was created for a touring company — in this case the Alice Nielsen Opera Company — which accounted for its brief stay at Wallack's Theatre (then located at Broadway and 30th Street). It was the third and most celebrated of the 13 shows written together by composer Victor Herbert and lyricist-librettist Harry B. Smith (whose total Broadway output was an incredible 123 productions). The musical, which did much to establish Herbert as America's preeminent composer of operetta, makes use of the popular theme of mistaken identity. Hungarian heiress Irma loves a dashing Hussar, but is promised in marriage to a wealthy count. To avoid this unwanted union, Irma gets gypsy fortune teller Musette (both roles being played by Alice Nielsen) to substitute for her. Eventually — somehow aided by a Hungarian military victory — Irma and Musette end up with their appropriate inamoratos. In 1946, a Broadway musical, *Gypsy Lady,* combined this score with that of another Herbert-Smith work, *The Serenade.* The plot, however, was relatively original.

FLORODORA

Music:
Leslie Stuart

Lyrics:
Leslie Stuart, Paul Rubens, Frank Clement

Book:
Owen Hall

Producer:
Tom Ryley & John Fisher

Directors:
Lewis Hopper & Willie Edouin

Cast:
**Edna Wallace Hopper, Fannie Johnston,
Willie Edouin, Sydney Deane,
R.E. Graham, May Edouin**

Songs:
**"The Shade of the Palm" (Stuart);
"Tell Me, Pretty Maiden" (Stuart);
"When I Leave Town" (Rubens);
"I Want to Be a Military Man" (Clement)**

New York run:
Casino Theatre, November 12, 1900; 553 p.

Florodora. Pictured on the sheet music cover are the ladies of the original Sextette: Daisy Greene, Marjorie Relyea, Vaughn Texsmith, Margaret Walker, Agnes Wayburn, and Marie L. Wilson.

*N*ext to the Gilbert and Sullivan comic operas, *Florodora* was the most successful early British import staged in New York, even exceeding the original London run of 455 performances. The highlight of the show was the appearance of the dainty, parasol-twirling *Florodora* Sextette who, with six male partners, introduced the coquettish number, "Tell Me, Pretty Maiden." In the plotty plot, Florodora is both the name of an island in the Philippines and the locally manufactured perfume. The elderly manufacturer Cyrus Gilfain wants to marry Dolores, whose father had been cheated by Gilfain, but Dolores loves Gilfain's manager, whom Gilfain wants for his own daughter, even though she loves someone else. For some reason, everyone ends up in Wales where the complications get unknotted and the knots get properly tied. The Casino Theatre, which was torn down in 1930, stood at Broadway and 39th Street.

The last Broadway revival of *Florodora* occurred in 1920 and ran for 150 performances. Christie MacDonald, Eleanor Painter, Walter Woolf, and George Hassell were in the cast.

BABES IN TOYLAND

Music:
Victor Herbert

Lyrics & book:
Glen MacDonough

Producers:
Fred R. Hamlin & Julian Mitchell

Director-choreographer:
Julian Mitchell

Cast:
**William Norris, Mabel Barrison,
George Denham, Bessie Wynn**

Songs:
**"I Can't Do the Sum";
"Go to Sleep, Slumber Deep";
"Song of the Poet";
"March of the Toys";
"Toyland";
"Never Mind, Bo-Peep"**

New York run:
Majestic Theatre, October 13, 1903; 192 p.

Babes in Toyland. William Norris and Mabel Barrison, as the two babes, lead Mother Hubbard's children in singing "I Can't Do the Sum." (Byron)

*B*ecause of the popularity of *The Wizard of Oz,* producers Fred R. Hamlin and Julian Mitchell (who was Broadway's most prolific director of musicals with 78 shows to his credit) commissioned Victor Herbert and Glen MacDonough to come up with a successor, if not exactly a sequel, to follow their previous hit into the Majestic Theatre. Once again audiences were delighted with a fantasy about children that included a devastating storm, a frightening journey through the woods, and the eventual arrival at a mythical magical city, in this case substituting Toyland for the Emerald City. The book may have been no more than a serviceable variation, but the score — the second and most successful of the five collaborations between Herbert and MacDonough — was far superior to its predecessor's. Laurel and Hardy appeared in the 1934 screen version, and Ray Bolger and Ed Wynn were in the 1961 version.

LITTLE JOHNNY JONES

Music, lyrics & book:
George M. Cohan

Producer:
Sam H. Harris

Director:
George M. Cohan

Cast:
**George M. Cohan, Jerry Cohan,
Helen Cohan, Donald Brian,
Ethel Levey, Tom Lewis**

Songs:
**"The Yankee Doodle Boy";
"Give My Regards to Broadway";
"Life's a Funny Proposition After All"**

New York run:
Liberty Theatre, November 7, 1904; 52 p.

*G*eorge M. Cohan was cocky, straight-shooting, self-assured, quick-witted, fast-moving, naively patriotic—in short, the personification of the American spirit at the beginning of the 20th Century. He was also just about the most multi-talented man ever to hit Broadway, winning fame as an actor, composer, lyricist, librettist, playwright, director, and producer, with an output comprising 21 musicals and 20 plays.

Little Johnny Jones, Cohan's third musical and his first hit, had an initial run of less than two months at the Liberty Theatre (now a movie house on 42nd Street west of Times Square). After extensive revisions during the road tour, the show returned to New York twice in 1905 for a total run of 20 weeks. The musical was prompted by a newspaper article about Tod Sloan, an American jockey then in England. In Cohan's story, jockey Johnny Jones has gone to Britain to ride his horse Yankee Doodle in the Derby. Accused of throwing the race, Johnny discovers that he has been framed by an American gambler (played by the author's father, Jerry Cohan). With the help of a private detective, he clears his name and celebrates by singing and dancing "Give My Regards to Broadway" on a Southampton pier. In the third act, with the locale abruptly switched to San Francisco's Chinatown, Johnny discovers that his fiancee, Goldie Gates (played by Ethel Levey, Cohan's wife at the time) has been kidnapped. When the jockey and the private detective apprehend the abductor, he turns out to be the same villain who had framed our hero in England. In 1982, a revival of *Little Johnny Jones* with Donny Osmond tarried but one night on Broadway.

MADEMOISELLE MODISTE

Music:
Victor Herbert

Lyrics & book:
Henry Blossom

Producer:
Charles Dillingham

Director:
Fred Latham

Cast:
**Fritzi Scheff, Walter Percival,
William Pruette, Claude Gillingwater,
Josephine Bartlett**

Songs:
**"Kiss Me Again";
"The Time, the Place and the Girl";
"I Want What I Want When I Want It";
"The Mascot of the Troop"**

New York run:
**Knickerbocker Theatre,
December 25, 1905; 202 p.**

Mlle. Modiste. Fritzi Scheff in the final scene at the charity bazaar in the gardens of the Chateau de St. Mar. From the left are Walter Percival (in uniform), William Pruette, and Claude Gillingwater. (Byron)

Mlle. Modiste inaugurated the partnership of composer Victor Herbert and librettist-lyricist Henry Blossom (they wrote eight scores together), and was their second in popularity to *The Red Mill.* The operetta was closely identified with prima donna Fritzi Scheff, who would be called upon to sing "Kiss Me Again" for the rest of her life (indeed, Miss Scheff returned to New York in *Mlle. Modiste* on five occasions, the last, when she was 50, in 1929). The musical, which opened at the Knickerbocker (then on Broadway and 38th Street), spins a Cinderella tale of a stagestruck Parisian named Fifi, who works in Mme. Cecile's hat shop on the Rue de la Paix. A wealthy American helps Fifi become a celebrated singer, which also helps smooth the way to her winning the approval of her sweetheart's aristocratic, crotchety uncle.

FORTY-FIVE MINUTES FROM BROADWAY

Music, lyrics & book:
George M. Cohan

Producers:
Marc Klaw & A. L. Erlanger

Director:
George M. Cohan

Cast:
**Fay Templeton, Victor Moore,
Donald Brian, Lois Ewell**

Songs:
**"I Want to Be a Popular Millionaire";
"Mary's a Grand Old Name";
"So Long, Mary";
"Forty-five Minutes from Broadway"**

New York run:
**New Amsterdam Theatre,
January 1, 1906; 90 p.**

Forty-five Minutes from Broadway. The dramatic will-tearing scene with Victor Moore and Fay Templeton. (Hall)

*M*ore of a play with music than a musical comedy — there were only five songs in the score — *Forty-five Minutes from Broadway* was written as a vehicle for Fay Templeton, but it was Victor Moore, in his first leading role on Broadway, who stole everyone's attention. In the story, set in New Rochelle, New York — which is only 45 minutes from Broadway — a nasty millionaire has died leaving a will that no one can find. His nephew (Donald Brian), who has been assigned as his heir, visits his uncle's home with his secretary, Kid Burns (Mr. Moore), and his fiancee. Burns discovers the will — and the fact that everything has been left to housekeeper Mary Jane Jenkins (Miss Templeton). Since the Kid has fallen in love with Mary, his pride won't let him marry his beloved for her money. The only solution: Mary tears up the will. After only a modest run at the New Amsterdam (now a movie house on 42nd Street west of Times Square), the show became a hit on the road, then was revived in 1912 with Cohan himself taking over the Kid Burns part. Moore, however, again played the same character in Cohan's 1907 musical, *The Talk of New York*.

THE RED MILL

Music:
Victor Herbert

Lyrics & book:
Henry Blossom

Producer:
Charles Dillingham

Director:
Fred Latham

Cast:
**David Montgomery, Fred Stone,
Augusta Greenleaf, Joseph Ratliff,
Allene Crater, Edward Begley**

Songs:
**"The Isle of Our Dreams";
"When You're Pretty and the World Is Fair";
"Moonbeams";
"Every Day Is Ladies Day With Me";
"The Streets of New York";
"Because You're You"**

New York run:
**Knickerbocker Theatre,
September 24, 1906; 274 p.**

The Red Mill was closer to being a musical farce than the kind of operetta usually associated with Victor Herbert. There was ample compensation, however, in the fact that it achieved the longest run of any of the composer's 41 book musicals produced during his lifetime. The show, which was typical of many of the period in depicting Americans as innocents abroad, is concerned with the adventures of Kid Conner and Con Kidder (Montgomery and Stone), two impoverished tourists stranded in Katwyk-aan-Zee, Holland. Their comic predicaments force them to don a number of disguises (including Sherlock Holmes and Dr. Watson), and they also manage to rescue a girl from a windmill by perching her precariously on one of the sails.

A 1945 production ran almost twice as long as the original, with Eddie Foy scoring a hit in the Dave Montgomery part. Also associated with the show were Stone's two daughters, co-producer Paula and featured actress Dorothy. The favorable reception that greeted this version sparked revivals of two other vintage shows as vehicles for major comedians: *Sweethearts* with Bobby Clark (1947) and *Sally* with Willie Howard (1948).

THE MERRY WIDOW

Music:
Franz Lehár

Lyrics:
Adrian Ross

Book:
(Basil Hood uncredited)

Producer:
Henry W. Savage

Director:
George Marion

Cast:
**Ethel Jackson, Donald Brian,
Lois Ewell, R.E. Graham,
William Weedon, Fred Frear**

Songs:
**"A Dutiful Wife";
"In Marsovia";
"Oh, Come Away, Away!";
"Maxim's";
"Vilia";
"Silly, Silly Cavalier";
"I Love You So" ("The Merry Widow Waltz");
"The Girls at Maxim's";
"Love in My Heart"**

New York run:
**New Amsterdam Theatre,
October 21, 1907; 416 p.**

*T*he epitome of the lighthearted, melodious, romantic European operetta, Franz Lehár's *The Merry Widow* first swirled onto the stage in Vienna in 1905 under the title *Die Lusbge Witwe.* The original text by Viktor Leon and Leo Stein was adapted for the highly successful London production by Basil Hood who refused program credit to spare the feelings of the original librettist whose work had been rejected. This version was also used in New York where the musical won such acclaim that it not only made celebrities of Ethel Jackson and Donald Brian, as the Widow and the Prince, it also prompted the introduction of Merry Widow hats, gowns, corsets, and cigarettes.

The first theatrical offshoot was a parody, *The Merry Widow Burlesque,* which opened less than three months after the operetta's première and continued for 156 performances. Producer Joe Weber (of Weber and Fields) even managed to get permission to use the Lehár music. A more lasting influence, however, was the rash of imported continental operettas that remained a major part of the Broadway scene until the outbreak of World War 1. Among the most popular of these were Oscar Straus's *A Waltz Dream,* Leo Fall's *The Dollar Princess,* Straus's *The Chocolate Soldier,* Heinrich Reinhardt's *The Spring Maid,* Johann Strauss's *The Merry Countess (Die Fledermaus),* Lehár's *The Count of Luxembourg,* Emmerich Kalman's *Sari,* and Edmund Eysler's *The Blue Paradise* (with interpolated songs by Sigmund Romberg).

Based on *L'Attaché d'Ambassade,* a French play by Henri Meilhac, *The Merry Widow* is set in Paris and concerns the efforts of Baron Popoff, the ambassador of the mythical kingdom of Marsovia, to induce his attaché, Prince Danilo, to marry wealthy widow Sonia Sadoya in order to aid the country's dwindling finances. Though the widow is wary of fortune-hunting suitors and the prince is chary of being taken for one, they find themselves falling in love to the seductive strains of "The Merry Widow Waltz." Danilo eventually proposes marriage — but only after Sonia has teasingly confessed that she has no money.

The Merry Widow has had five Broadway revivals, the last in 1943. That production, with a libretto coauthored by novelist Sidney Sheldon, had a successful run of 322 performances, then returned in October 1944 for an additional 32. The cast was headed by the husband-wife team of Jan Kiepura and Marta Eggerth. In 1964, the operetta was mounted by the Music Theatre of Lincoln Center (with Patrice Munsel and Bob Wright), and in 1978 by the New York City Opera (with Beverly Sills and Alan Titus). There have been three Hollywood screen versions: a silent in 1925 directed by Erich Von Stroheim; the Ernst Lubitsch treatment in 1934 with lyrics by Lorenz Hart and starring Maurice Chevalier and Jeanette MacDonald; and a 1952 remake with Lana Turner and Fernando Lamas.

THE CHOCOLATE SOLDIER

Music:
Oscar Straus

Lyrics & book:
Stanislaus Stange

Producer:
Fred C. Whitney

Director:
Stanislaus Stange

Choreographer:
Al Holbrook

Cast:
**Ida Brooks Hunt, J.E. Gardner,
Flavia Arcaro, William Pruette**

Songs:
**"My Hero";
"Sympathy";
"Seek the Spy";
"That Would Be Lovely";
"Falling In Love";
"The Letter Song";
"Thank the Lord the War Is Over"**

New York run:
Lyric Theatre, September 13, 1909; 296 p.

*O*f all the European operettas imported by Broadway producers in the wake of the spectacular success of *The Merry Widow,* by far the most popular was *The Chocolate Soldier.* Originally presented in Vienna in 1908 as *Der Tapfere Soldat,* the musical was adapted from George Bernard Shaw's play, *Arms and the Man* though the author always regretted having given his permission. (The next musical treatment of a Shaw play, *My Fair Lady,* came along 47 years later.)

Producer Fred Whitney secured the rights to the English-language version even before the operetta had had its première at the Theater an der Wien, and he opened it in New York at the Lyric Theatre (now a movie house on 42nd Street west of Times Square). The satire on heroes and heroism is set in 1885 during the Serbian invasion of Bulgaria. Lt. Bumerli, the chocolate-eating Swiss soldier serving in the Serb army, is more concerned about saving his neck than displaying valor on the battlefield. He hides in the home of Col. Popoff, a Bulgarian, and soon meets Popoff's daughter, Nadina. Though Nadina's hero is the swaggering Major Alexius Spiridoff, it is not long before she drops him for the peace-loving Bumerli. Other Broadway productions of *The Chocolate Soldier* were offered in 1921, 1930, 1931, 1934, and 1947 (the last in a revised version by Guy Bolton). The 1941 movie with Rise Stevens and Nelson Eddy used a different story.

MADAME SHERRY

Music:
Karl Hoschna

Lyrics & book:
Otto Harbach

Producers:
A. H. Woods, H. H. Frazee, George Lederer

Director:
George Lederer

Cast:
**Lina Abarbanell, Ralph Herz,
Elizabeth Murray, Jack Gardner,
Dorothy Jardon, Frances Demarest**

Songs:
**"Every Little Movement"; "The Smile
She Meant for Me"; "I Want to Play House
With You"; "The Birth of Passion"; "Put Your
Arms Around Me Honey" (Albert Von Tilzer -
Junie McCree)**

New York run:
**New Amsterdam Theatre,
August 30, 1910; 231 p.**

Madame Sherry remains the best remembered of the six productions written by Karl Hoschna and Otto Harbach (who spelled his name Hauerbach until World War 1). It was adapted from an English musical of 1903, which had a different score, and which, in turn, had been based on a French musical. Among the reasons for its success were the insinuating number, "Every Little Movement" (" . . . has a meaning all its own") and the interpolated "Put Your Arms Around Me Honey." In this tangled tale of mistaken identity, Ed Sherry deceives his uncle, wealthy archaeologist Theophilus Sherry, into accepting his Irish landlady as his wife and a dancing teacher's pupils as their children. At first Ed is smitten with Lulu, the dancing teacher, but then transfers his affections to Yvonne, his cousin (played by Metropolitan opera diva Lina Abarbanell). Audiences could enjoy matinee performances of *Madame Sherry* for a top ticket price of $1.50.

NAUGHTY MARIETTA

Music:
Victor Herbert

Lyrics & book:
Rida Johnson Young

Producer:
Oscar Hammerstein

Director:
Jacques Coini

Cast:
**Emma Trentini, Orville Harrold,
Edward Martindel, Marie Duchene,
Peggy Wood**

Songs:
**"Tramp! Tramp! Tramp";
"Naughty Marietta";
"'Neath the Southern Moon";
"Italian Street Song";
"Live for Today";
"I'm Falling in Love With Someone";
"Ah! Sweet Mystery of Life"**

New York run:
New York Theatre, November 7, 1910; 136 p.

*V*ictor Herbert's crowning achievement came into being because mounting debts had forced opera impresario Oscar Hammerstein (grandfather of Oscar II) into the area of the more commercial musical theatre. Hammerstein had it staged with all the care of one of his Manhattan Opera productions, with two of his stars, Emma Trentini and Orville Harrold, in the leading roles of Marietta d'Altena and Capt. Dick Warrington.

Naughty Marietta takes place in New Orleans in 1780. Marietta is there to escape from an unwanted marriage in France and Capt. Dick is there to lead his Rangers against a pirate gang led by Bras Pique ("Tattooed Arm"). Though Marietta is first attracted to Etienne Grandet, the son of the lieutenant governor, when he is revealed as the pirate leader she is happy to sing her romantic duets with Capt. Dick. She is, in fact, sure that he is the man for her because he is able to finish the "Dream Melody" ("Ah! Sweet Mystery of Life") that Marietta recalls from childhood. One historical error committed by the authors is that New Orleans is supposed to be a French posession, whereas in the year in which the story takes place the colony belonged to Spain. (This error was also made in *The New Moon* in 1928, which had the same locale and period.) The 1935 movie version co-starred Jeanette MacDonald and Nelson Eddy.

THE PINK LADY

Music:
Ivan Caryll

Lyrics & book:
C. M. S. McLellan

Producers:
Marc Klaw & A. L. Erlanger

Director:
Herbert Gresham

Choreographer:
Julian Mitchell

Cast:
**Hazel Dawn, Alice Dovey, William Elliott,
Frank Lalor, Jed Prouty**

Songs:
**"On the Saskatchewan";
"My Beautiful Lady";
"Hide and Seek";
"Donny Did, Donny Didn't"**

New York run:
**New Amsterdam Theatre,
March 13, 1911; 312 p.**

*A*fter winning success in London, composer Ivan Caryll indited the scores for 14 Broadway musicals. His most celebrated production was *The Pink Lady,* which contained the durable song "My Beautiful Lady" and gave Hazel Dawn a memorable role that allowed her to play the violin. The story, adapted from a French play, *Le Satyr,* takes place in one day, during which we visit a restaurant in the woods at Compiègne, a furniture shop on the Rue Honoré, and the Ball of the Nymphs and Satyrs. Before settling down to marriage with Angele, Lucien Garidel hopes to enjoy one last fling with Claudine (Miss Dawn), known as the Pink Lady because of her monochromatic wardrobe. When they accidentally meet Angele, Lucien covers his embarrassment by introducing Claudine as the wife of a friend. Following comic complications, the day ends with the involved couples properly sorted.

THE FIREFLY

Music:
Rudolf Friml

Lyrics & book:
Otto Harbach

Producer:
Arthur Hammerstein

Director:
Fred Latham

Choreographer:
Signor Albertieri, Sammy Lee

Cast:
**Emma Trentini, Craig Campbell,
Roy Atwell, Sammy Lee,
Audrey Maple, Melville Stewart**

Songs:
**"Giannina Mia";
"When a Maid Comes Knocking at Your
Heart";
"Love Is Like a Firefly";
"Sympathy"**

New York run:
Lyric Theatre, December 2, 1912; 120 p.

*D*uring a performance he was conducting of *Naughty Marietta,* Victor Herbert had a disagreement with the star, Emma Trentini, and stormed off the podium. He also refused to have anything to do with her next vehicle, *The Firefly,* for which he had been contracted. The composer's decision opened the way for Rudolf Friml, who had never written a Broadway score before, to become a leading creator of American operettas. It also began his partnership with librettist-lyricist Otto Harbach, with whom he would be associated on ten musicals. In the Cinderella tale, cut from a similar bolt of cloth as the one used for *Mlle. Modiste,* Nina Corelli, an Italian street singer in New York, disguises herself as a cabin boy to be near Jack Travers, a guest on a yacht sailing for Bermuda. After hearing her sing, a music teacher offers to give her lessons, and within three years she becomes both a renowned prima donna and Mrs. Jack Travers.

SWEETHEARTS

Music:
Victor Herbert

Lyrics:
Robert B. Smith

Book:
Harry B. Smith & Fred De Gresac

Producers:
Louis Werba & Mark Luescher

Director:
Fred Latham

Choreographer:
Charles Morgan Jr.

Cast:
**Christie MacDonald, Thomas Conkey,
Ethel Du Fre Houston, Edwin Wilson,
Tom McNaughton**

Songs:
**"Sweethearts";
"Angelus";
"Every Lover Must Meet His Fate";
"Pretty as a Picture";
"Jeannette and Her Little Wooden Shoes"**

New York run:
**New Amsterdam Theatre,
September 8, 1913; 136 p.**

*T*hough allegedly based on the real-life adventures of a 15th Century Neapolitan princess, *Sweethearts* was easily among Broadway's most farfetched musical romances, complete with a mythological country, an abducted princess, and a prince in disguise. To keep her from harm during a war, the infant Princess Sylvia of Zilania has been taken to Bruges where she is brought up believing she is the daughter of a laundress. While traveling incognito, Prince Franz falls in love with Sylvia even before they meet. After their true identities are revealed, they assume the throne as King and Queen of Zilania.

Prompted by the successful 1945 revival of Herbert's *The Red Mill* starring comic Eddie Foy Jr., Herbert's *Sweethearts* was resuscitated for comic Bobby Clark. Here the secondary role of political operator Mikel Mikeloviz was retailored to Clark's specifications, and the resourceful clown turned the evening into a self-kidding, hilarious romp. The run was almost twice as long as the original. The 1938 Jeanette MacDonald-Nelson Eddy movie version had a different story.

THE GIRL FROM UTAH

Music:
Jerome Kern, etc.

Lyrics:
Harry B. Smith, etc.

Book:
James T. Tanner, Harry B. Smith

Producer:
Charles Frohman

Director:
J. A. E. Malone

Cast:
Julia Sanderson, Donald Brian,
Joseph Cawthorn, Queenie Vassar,
Venita Fitzhugh

Songs:
"Same Sort of Girl"; "They Didn't Believe Me"
(lyric: Herbert Reynolds); "Gilbert the Filbert"
(Herman Finck - Arthur Wimperis);
"Why Don't They Dance the Polka?";
"The Land of Let's Pretend"

New York run:
Knickerbocker Theatre,
August 24, 1914; 120 p.

*B*ased on a 1913 London musical with music by Paul Rubens and Sidney Jones and lyrics by Adrian Ross and Percy Greenbank, *The Girl from Utah* underwent a major sea change by the time it opened on Broadway, with no less than seven songs now credited to Jerome Kern (including his first hit, "They Didn't Believe Me"). Despite the somewhat misleading title, the story is set in London where Una Trance (Julia Sanderson) has fled to avoid marrying a bigamist Mormon. Though the Mormon pursues her, Una eventually finds true love in the arms of Sandy Blair (Donald Brian), a London song-and-dance man. The show was the first musical hit on Broadway following the outbreak of World War I. With its appealing Kern additions (it was the composer's sixth of 39 Broadway shows), the production was a transitional work leading to the soon-to-come American domination of the musical-comedy field.

WATCH YOUR STEP

Music & lyrics:
Irving Berlin

Book:
Harry B. Smith

Producer:
Charles Dillingham

Director:
R. H. Burnside

Cast:
Vernon & Irene Castle, Frank Tinney,
Charles King, Elizabeth Brice,
Elizabeth Murray, Harry Kelly,
Justine Johnstone

Songs:
"Play a Simple Melody";
"They Always Follow Me Around";
"When I Discovered You";
"Settle Down in a One-Horse Town";
"The Syncopated Walk"

New York run:
New Amsterdam Theatre,
December 8, 1914; 175 p.

*I*n 1911, at the age of 23, Irving Berlin had the entire country ragtime crazy with "Alexander's Ragtime Band." Three years later, he wrote his first Broadway score (out of a total of 21) which was the first to feature ragtime. It also introduced audiences to another Berlin skill in the contrapuntal "Play a Simple Melody." The songs accompanied a vehicle for dancers Vernon and Irene Castle (it would be the couple's last professional appearance together) that was so flimsy the program credit line read, "Plot, if any, by Harry B. Smith." That plot had to do with a will leaving $2 million to anyone who had never been in love, but by the second act the story was discarded and the evening was turned into a facsimile of a Fifth Avenue nightclub floor show. Also discarded was W.C. Fields. Then primarily a juggler, Fields had sailed from Australia to join the cast during the Syracuse tryout, only to be fired after one performance. The reason: producer Dillingham was fearful that Fields would be such a hit that audiences wouldn't pay attention to the Castles.

As sung by Mr. CHAS. E. KNORR.

Oh promise me.

Words by CLEMENT SCOTT.

R. de KOVEN, Op. 50.

Moderato.

THE BOWERY.

Words by CHAS. H. HOYT.   **Music by PERCY GAUNT.**

blaze with lights; I..... had one of the dev-il's own
hands on me!" "Get off the Bow-'ry you Yep!" said
it to me,— "I sold you the box, not the socks," said
out," said she; A man called a bounc-er at-tend-ed to
most of my chin; That was the worst scrape I ev-er got
down!" said I; Then.... he laughed, tho' I could-'nt see

nights! I'll nev - er go there a - - ny more!.........
he, I'll nev - er go there a - - ny more!.........
he, I'll nev - er go there a - - ny more!.........
me, I'll nev - er go there a - - ny more!.........
in, I'll nev - er go there a - - ny more!.........
why! I'll nev - er go there a - - ny more!.........

CHORUS.

The Bow - - - 'ry, the Bow - - - - 'ry! They

After the Ball.

Arr. by JOS. CLAUDER.

Words and Music by CHAS. K. HARRIS.

1. A lit - tle maid - - en climbed an old man's knee............
2. Bright lights were flash - - ing in the grand ball - room,..........
3. Long years have passed child,.......... I've nev - er wed,............

Begged for a sto - ry- "Do Un - cle please.".........
Soft ly the mu - sic, play - ing sweet tunes............
True to my lost love, though she is dead.........

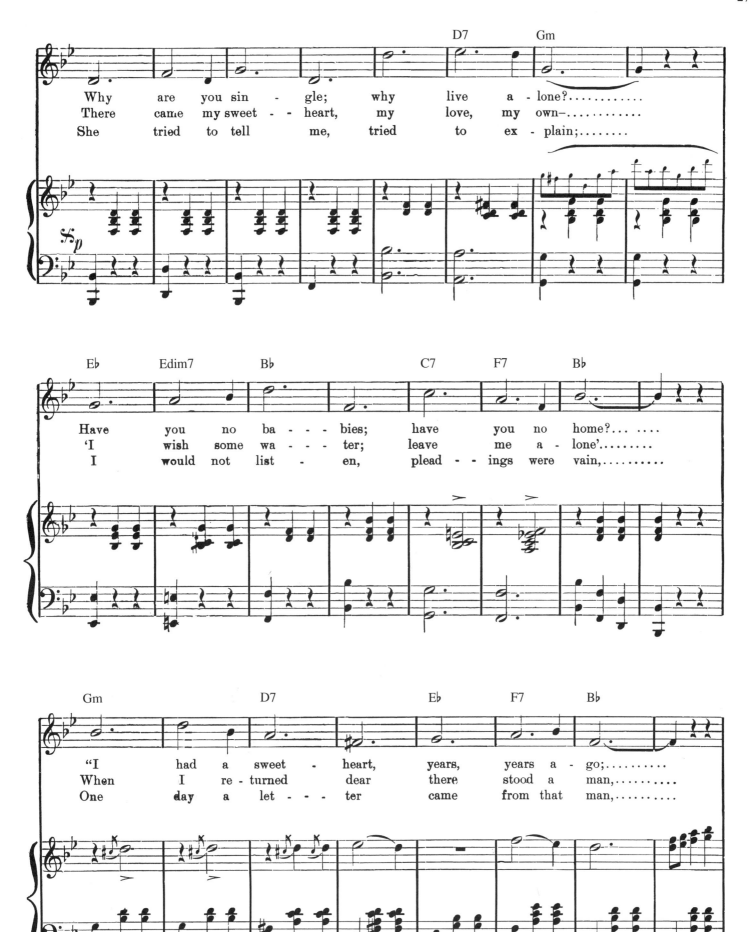

Why are you sin - gle; why live a - lone?............
There came my sweet - - heart, my love, my own—............
She tried to tell me, tried to ex - plain;........

Have you no ba - - - bies; have you no home?.... ....
'I wish some wa - - - ter; leave me a - lone'........
I would not list - en, plead - - ings were vain,..........

"I had a sweet - heart, years, years a - go;..........
When I re - turned dear there stood a man,..........
One day a let - - - ter came from that man,..........

Where she is now pet, you will soon know........
Kiss - ing my sweet - heart as lov - ers can........
He was her broth - er— the let - ter ran........

List to the sto - ry, I'll tell it all,.........
Down fell the glass pet, brok - - en, that's all,.........
That's why I'm lone - ly, no home at all;.........

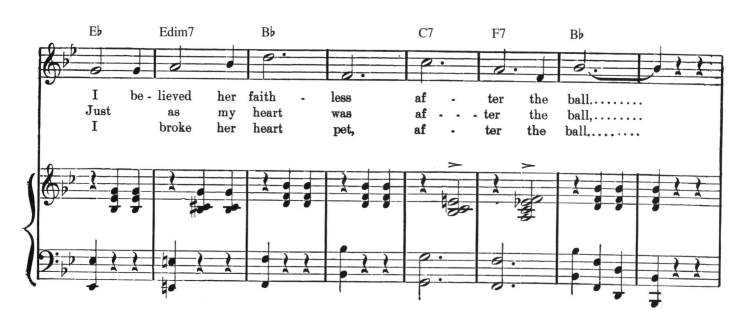

I be - lieved her faith - less af - ter the ball........
Just as my heart was af - - - ter the ball,........
I broke her heart pet, af - ter the ball........

Romany Life.
(Song a là Czardas.)

Words by HARRY B. SMITH.

Music by VICTOR HERBERT.

We have a home 'neath the for-est shades, Nev-er an-y oth-er _____ have we. _____ Nev-er an-y oth-er ___ have we. _____ Our camp - fires glow in the nooks and glades, Where our tents are white _____ to

GYPSY LOVE SONG.

(Slumber on, my little gypsy sweetheart.)

Words by Harry B. Smith.

Music by Victor Herbert.

Baritone and Mezzo Bass in A.

Tell Me Pretty Maiden.

English Girls and Clerks.

Moderato.

By LESLIE STUART.

44

must love some one, real-ly And it might as well be you!
must love some one, real-ly And it might as well be you!

March of the Toys

from

"Babes in Toyland."

by VICTOR HERBERT.

Allegro molto moderato sempre pesante.

Toyland.

Tom, Tom.

Lyric by
GLEN MAC DONOUGH.

Music by
VICTOR HERBERT.

"The Yankee Doodle Boy."

Tempo di Marcia.

GEO. M. COHAN.

I'm the kid that's all the can-dy,
Fa-ther's name was Hez - i - ki - ah,

I'm a Yan - kee Doo - dle Dan - dy, I'm glad I am, ___
Moth - er's name was Ann Ma - ri - a, Yanks through and through.

CHORUS.

I'm a Yan - kee Doo - dle Dan - - dy, A Yan - kee Doo - dle, do or die; _____ A real live nep - hew of my Un - cle Sam's, Born on the Fourth of Ju - ly. _____ I've

"Give My Regards To Broadway."

Tempo di Marcia.

GEO. M. COHAN.

CHORUS.

Give my re - gards to Broad - way, re -

mem - ber me to Her - ald Square,_____

Tell all the gang at For - ty - Sec - ond street, that

I will soon be there;_____

Kiss Me Again

Fifi.

Lyric by
HENRY BLOSSOM.

Music by
VICTOR HERBERT.

Valse lente.

Sweet sum-mer breeze, whis-per-ing trees, Stars shin-ing soft-ly a-bove;____ Ros-es in bloom, waft-ed per-fume, Sleep-y birds dream-ing of love.____ Safe in your arms, far from a-larms,

I Want What I Want When I Want It.

Lyric by
HENRY BLOSSOM.

Music by
VICTOR HERBERT.

"Mary's A Grand Old Name."

GEO. M. COHAN.

she called me Ma - ry, too.____ She was - n't gay or
she'll sure - ly bleach her hair.____ Though Ma - ry's or - di -

air - y, but plain as she could be; ____
na - ry, Ma - rie is fair to see; ____

I hate to meet a fair - y who calls her-self Ma - rie.____
Don't ev - er fear sweet Ma - ry, be-ware of sweet Ma - rie.____

CHORUS Slowly

For it is Ma - ry, Ma - ry, plain as a - ny name can

"Forty-five Minutes from Broadway."

Tempo di Valse.

GEO. M. COHAN.

brings; _____ For the short time it takes, what a diff'rence it makes In the
town; _____ Oh! the place is a bird, no one here ev-er heard Of Del-

ways of the peo-ple and things. _____ Oh! what a fine bunch of ru-
mon-i-co, Rec-tor or Browne. _____ With a ten dol-lar bill you're a spend-

bens, Oh! what a jay at-mos-phere; _____ They have whiskers like hay, and im-
thrift; if you o-pen a bot-tle of beer _____ You're a sport so they say, and im-

ag-ine Broadway on-ly for-ty-five minutes from here. _____ On-ly here. _____
ag-ine Broadway on-ly for-ty-five minutes from here. _____ On-ly here. _____

"The Isle of our Dreams"

Doris and Gretchen.

Words by
HENRY BLOSSOM.

Music by
VICTOR HERBERT.

"Every Day Is Ladies' Day With Me"

Words by
HENRY BLOSSOM.

Music by
VICTOR HERBERT

I should like, with-out un-due re-it-er-a-tion of the e - go, To ex-
It's a frightfull thing to think of all the hearts that I have broken, Al-tho'

plain, how ve - ry hard I find it is to make my pay go 'Round a-
each one fell in love with me with - out the slight - est to - ken, That my

mong my vul-gar cre-dit-ors I'm fear-ful-ly in debt, For I al-ways have af-ford-ed an-y-
fa - tal gift of beau-ty had in-flamed her lit-tle heart, But I found that some small fa-vor al-ways

The Streets of New York.

Con , Kid and Chorus.

Lyric by
HENRY BLOSSOM.

Music by.
VICTOR HERBERT.

Dance.

VILIA
Song

Words by
ADRIAN ROSS

Music by
FRANZ LEHAR
Arranged for the Piano by
H.M.HIGGS.

Allegretto

once was a Vil - ia, A witch of the wood, A hunt - er be-

held her a - lone as she stood. The spell of her beau - ty up-

-on him was laid; He look'd and he long'd for the mag - ic - al maid!

For a sud-den trem - or ran, Right thro' the love-be-wil - der'd man,

And he sigh'd as a hapless lov-er can. "Vil - ia, O Vil - ia! 'he

witch of the wood! Would I not die for you, dear, if I could?

Allegretto

The wood-maid-en smiled, and no an-swer she gave, But beck-on'd him in-to the shade of the cave; He nev-er had known such a rap-tur-ous bliss, No maid-en of mor-tals so sweet-ly can kiss!

I LOVE YOU SO!
Valse Song

Words by
ADRIAN ROSS.

Arr. for Piano by H. M. HIGGS
On Melodies by Franz Lehár.

Oh, Fatherland

or

"To Maxim's Then I Go."

(Da geh' ich zu Maxim's.)

Translations by
GEORGE BONIFACE.

German Lyrics by
VICTOR LEON & LEO STEIN.
Music by FRANZ LEHÁR.

Fa-ther-land you cause by day a lot of trou-ble and dis-may, But
Va-ter-land, du machst bei Tag mir schon ge-nü-gend Müh' und Plag'! Die

night leads me, a dip-lo-mat, to serve my-self, I'm good at that! For
Nacht braucht je-der Di-plo-mat doch meis-ten-teils für sich pri-vat! Um

My Hero

English words by
STANISLAUS STANGE

Music by
OSCAR STRAUS

113

"Put Your Arms Around Me, Honey"

(I Never Knew Any Girl Like You.)

Words by
JUNIE McCREE.

Music by
ALBERT VON TILZER.

it's with you dear, That I love to be.____

moon - y, loon - y, But my love' is true.____

CHORUS.

Put your arms a - round me hon - ey, hold me tight,

Hud - dle up and cud - dle up with all your might,

Oh, babe, Won't you roll dem eyes, Eyes that

Every Little Movement.

Lulu and Leonard.

Lyric by
O. A. HAUERBACH.

Music by
KARL HOSCHNA.

REFRAIN. *Moderato grazioso.*

Ev - 'ry lit-tle move-ment has a mean - ing all its own,

Ev - 'ry tho't and feel-ing by some pos - ture can be shown, And ev-'ry

love tho't That comes a steal-ing O'er your be-ing__ must be re - veal-ing, All its

sweet-ness__ in some ap-peal-ing Lit-tle ges-ture__ all all its own.

Tramp! Tramp! Tramp!

Lyric by
RIDA JOHNSON YOUNG

Music by
VICTOR HERBERT

Allegro marcato

We've hunt - ed the wolf in the for - est, We've
We've ranged o'er the North in the win - ter, We've

raid - ed the pi - rates at sea,____ We have no in - den - ture, we're
an - swered the call of the wild,____ We heard the wolf call - ing when

Italian Street Song.

Marietta and Chorus.

Lyric by
RIDA JOHNSON YOUNG.

Music by
VICTOR HERBERT.

Allegro moderato.

I'm Falling In Love With Some One.

Captain Dick.

Lyric by
RIDA JOHNSON YOUNG.

Music by
VICTOR HERBERT.

Ah! Sweet Mystery Of Life.

(The Dream Melody.)

Lyric by
RIDA JOHNSON YOUNG.

Music by
VICTOR HERBERT.

MY BEAUTIFUL LADY.

Words by C. M. S. McLELLAN.   Music by IVAN CARYLL.

Tempo di Valse

To you, beau-ti-ful la-dy, I raise my eyes,

My heart, beau-ti-ful la-dy, to your heart sighs,

Come, come, beau-ti-ful la-dy, to Par - a - dise,.......... E're the

sweet, sweet waltz dream dies.

Giannina mia

Nina

Words by
Otto Hauerbach

From the Comedy-Opera
"The Firefly," by
Rudolf Friml

Sympathy

WALTZ-SONG
From the Comedy-Opera "The Firefly"

Otto Hauerbach

Geraldine and Thurston

Rudolf Friml

REFRAIN

Sweethearts

Lyrics by
Robert B. Smith

From the Comic Opera
"Sweethearts," by
Victor Herbert

Seek the dwell-ing of two hap-py sweet-hearts, You will find it there!

Sweet-hearts make love their ver-y own, Sweet-hearts can live on love a-lone,

For them the eyes where love-light lies O-pen the gates to Par-a-dise! All oth-er

love is doomed to fade, It is like sun-shine veiled in shade, Such joys of

life as love im-parts Are all of them yours, sweet-hearts!

They Didn't Believe Me.

Words by
HERBERT REYNOLDS

Music by
JEROME KERN.

Simple Melody

Ernesta, Algy and Chorus

Words and Music
by IRVING BERLIN

back the rhymes of old-en times And just for old times sake.
why I long to hear a song Like moth-er used to sing.

Rag Version

Mu-si-cal De-mon, set your hon-ey a dream-in, won't you play me some rag,

Won't you play a simp-le mel - o-

Just change that class-ie-al nag To some sweet beau-ti-ful drag If you will

dy ___ Like my moth-er sang to me ___

BROADWAY MUSICALS
Show by Show

THIS UNIQUE SERIES EXPLORES BROADWAY'S BIGGEST HITS YEAR BY YEAR AND SHOW BY SHOW. INTERESTING FACTS AND TRIVIA AS WELL AS ARRANGEMENTS FOR THE BEST SONGS FROM EACH SHOW ARE PRESENTED IN A PACKAGE NO BROADWAY FAN CAN RESIST! THE TEXT ABOUT THE SHOWS WAS WRITTEN BY RENOWNED BROADWAY HISTORIAN STANLEY GREEN, AND IS DRAWN FROM HIS BOOK *BROADWAY MUSICALS SHOW BY SHOW*. THIS IS DEFINITELY THE ULTIMATE COLLECTION OF BROADWAY MUSIC AND HISTORY — BE SURE TO COLLECT THE WHOLE SERIES!

BROADWAY MUSICALS SHOW BY SHOW 1891 - 1916
33 CLASSICS FROM SHOWS SUCH AS: *ROBIN HOOD, FLORODORA, BABES IN TOYLAND, THE MERRY WIDOW,* AND MORE. SONGS INCLUDE: AFTER THE BALL • THE BOWERY • GIVE MY REGARDS TO BROADWAY • I LOVE YOU SO! (THE MERRY WIDOW WALTZ) • THE ISLE OF OUR DREAMS • KISS ME AGAIN • MARCH OF THE TOYS • MARY'S A GRAND OLD NAME • MY HERO • SIMPLE MELODY • STREETS OF NEW YORK • TOYLAND • AND MORE.
00311514 $12.95

BROADWAY MUSICALS SHOW BY SHOW 1917 - 1929
OVER 40 SONGS FROM THE ERA'S MOST POPULAR SHOWS, INCLUDING: *ZIEGFELD FOLLIES, THE STUDENT PRINCE IN HEIDELBERG, NO NO NANETTE, OH, KAY!, SHOW BOAT, FIFTY MILLION FRENCHMEN,* AND MORE. SONGS INCLUDE: THE BIRTH OF THE BLUES • CAN'T HELP LOVIN' DAT MAN • FASCINATING RHYTHM • HOW LONG HAS THIS BEEN GOING ON? • I'M JUST WILD ABOUT HARRY • OL' MAN RIVER • A PRETTY GIRL IS LIKE A MELODY • ST. LOUIS BLUES • SECOND HAND ROSE • TEA FOR TWO • YOU DO SOMETHING TO ME • YOU'RE THE CREAM IN MY COFFEE • AND MORE.
00311515 $14.95

BROADWAY MUSICALS SHOW BY SHOW 1950 - 1959
55 SONGS FROM SUCH CLASSICS AS *THE KING AND I, MY FAIR LADY, WEST SIDE STORY, GYPSY, THE SOUND OF MUSIC,* AND MORE. SONGS INCLUDE: DO-RE-MI • EDELWEISS • EVERYTHING'S COMING UP ROSES • GETTING TO KNOW YOU • I COULD HAVE DANCED ALL NIGHT • I'VE GROWN ACCUSTOMED TO HER FACE • LET ME ENTERTAIN YOU • LUCK BE A LADY • MACK THE KNIFE • MARIA • SEVENTY SIX TROMBONES • SHALL WE DANCE? • SOMEWHERE • WOULDN'T IT BE LOVERLY • AND MORE.
00311518 $14.95

BROADWAY MUSICALS SHOW BY SHOW 1960 - 1971
OVER 45 SONGS FROM SHOWS SUCH AS *OLIVER!, CABARET, CAMELOT, HELLO, DOLLY!, FIDDLER ON THE ROOF, JESUS CHRIST SUPERSTAR, MAME,* AND MORE. SONGS INCLUDE: AS LONG AS HE NEEDS ME • CONSIDER YOURSELF • DAY BY DAY • I DON'T KNOW HOW TO LOVE HIM • IF EVER I WOULD LEAVE YOU • IF I WERE A RICH MAN • PEOPLE • SUNRISE, SUNSET • TRY TO REMEMBER • WE NEED A LITTLE CHRISTMAS • WHAT KIND OF FOOL AM I? • AND MORE.
00311521 $14.95

BROADWAY MUSICALS SHOW BY SHOW 1930 - 1939
A COLLECTION OF OVER 45 SONGS FROM THE DECADE'S BIGGEST BROADWAY HITS, INCLUDING: *ANYTHING GOES, PORGY AND BESS, BABES IN ARMS, ON YOUR TOES* AND MORE. SONGS INCLUDE: BEGIN THE BEGUINE • EMBRACEABLE YOU • FALLING IN LOVE WITH LOVE • FRIENDSHIP • I GET A KICK OUT OF YOU • I GOT RHYTHM • THE LADY IS A TRAMP • MY FUNNY VALENTINE • MY HEART BELONGS TO DADDY • ON YOUR TOES • SMOKE GETS IN YOUR EYES • STRIKE UP THE BAND • SUMMERTIME • IT AIN'T NECESSARILY SO • AND MORE.
00311516 $14.95

BROADWAY MUSICALS SHOW BY SHOW 1940 - 1949
SHOW DESCRIPTIONS AND OVER 45 SONGS FROM THE BROADWAY HITS *PAL JOEY, OKLAHOMA!, CAROUSEL, ANNIE GET YOUR GUN, FINIAN'S RAINBOW, SOUTH PACIFIC* AND MORE. SONGS INCLUDE: ANOTHER OP'NIN, ANOTHER SHOW • BALI HAI • BEWITCHED • DIAMOND'S ARE A GIRL'S BEST FRIEND • IF I LOVED YOU • NEW YORK, NEW YORK • OH, WHAT A BEAUTIFUL MORNIN' • OLD DEVIL MOON • SOME ENCHANTED EVENING • THE SURREY WITH THE FRINGE ON TOP • YOU'LL NEVER WALK ALONE • MORE.
00311517 $14.95

BROADWAY MUSICALS SHOW BY SHOW 1972 - 1988
OVER 30 SONGS FROM THE ERA OF BIG PRODUCTIONS LIKE *PHANTOM OF THE OPERA, EVITA, LA CAGE AUX FOLLES, LES MISERABLES, ME AND MY GIRL, A CHORUS LINE, CATS* AND MORE. SONGS INCLUDE: ALL I ASK OF YOU • DON'T CRY FOR ME ARGENTINA • I AM WHAT I AM • I DREAMED A DREAM • THE LAMBETH WALK • MEMORY • THE MUSIC OF THE NIGHT • ON MY OWN • SEND IN THE CLOWNS • TOMORROW • WHAT I DID FOR LOVE • AND MORE.
00311519 $14.95

Prices, contents and availability subject to change without notice.

For more information, see your local music dealer, or write to:
Hal Leonard Publishing Corporation
P.O. Box 13819 Milwaukee, Wisconsin 53213